Navigating Grief While Raising a Special Needs Child

GRIEF AND GRACE

About the Author

Rakshanda Hassan is an IT consultant, a writer, mother, and advocate who has transformed her life's most profound challenges into powerful narratives of resilience and hope. Originally from India and now residing in Phoenix, Arizona, Rakshanda's life took a dramatic turn when her son was diagnosed with special needs at the age of three. Seven years later, she faced another devastating loss — the death of her husband — leaving her to navigate the complex terrain of grief while raising a special needs child alone.

Through her writing, Rakshanda candidly shares her journey of rebuilding a life that felt shattered, finding strength in the smallest moments, and discovering unexpected joy amidst profound loss. She is passionate about helping others facing similar struggles, encouraging them to embrace their pain, honor their stories, and find the courage to move forward.

When she isn't writing, Rakshanda finds solace in nature, quiet moments of reflection. This book is her heartfelt guidebook for those walking the delicate line between loss and love, reminding readers that even in the darkest moments, hope can be found.

Navigating Grief

Grief and Grace

Table of Contents:

WHY THIS GUIDE? PERSONAL STORY/EXPERIENCE 8

HOW TO USE THIS GUIDE: A PRACTICAL APPROACH 13

NAVIGATING GRIEF WHILE RAISING A SPECIAL NEEDS CHILD 15

CHAPTER 1: UNDERSTANDING GRIEF 17

FINDING ME AGAIN 26

MILESTONES AND MEMORY MARKERS 28

CHAPTER 2: THE OVERLAP OF GRIEF AND PARENTING 31

CHAPTER 4: FINDING PURPOSE AMIDST LOSS 52

CHAPTER 5: MINDFULNESS AND EMOTIONAL REGULATION 62

CHAPTER 6: NAVIGATING UNCERTAINTY AND FUTURE PLANNING 71

CHAPTER 7: FINDING MEANING AND REBUILDING IDENTITY 79

CHAPTER 8: ROMANTICIZE YOUR LIFE   92

CONCLUSION: A PATH FORWARD   94

Acknowledgments

To my family and friends — the ones who have held me through the darkest nights and reminded me that even in the midst of loss, love remains.

To my son, whose laughter continues to be the brightest light in my life. Your resilience and innocence have been my anchor, grounding me when the world felt like it was spinning out of control. You are the reason I keep moving forward, step by step, day by day.

To my late husband — your presence is felt in every word of this book. Though you are no longer physically here, your love and strength continue to guide me. You taught me what it means to love fiercely and to hold on even when life feels unbearably heavy.

To my mother, whose unwavering courage and warmth still echo in my heart. You were my first teacher in resilience, and your spirit continues to inspire me to be the kind of woman who can rise even when the world feels like it's crumbling.

To my close friends who became my chosen family — thank you for showing up, for sitting with me in the silence, for letting me cry, vent, and rage without judgment. You reminded me that even when words fail, presence is a language all its own.

To those who offered a kind word, a warm meal, a listening ear, or a comforting embrace — your small acts of kindness became lifelines in my moments of despair.

And to those who continue to walk this path with me, helping me find moments of joy, calm, and laughter amidst the grief — thank you for being the light when everything felt dark.

This book is not just my experiences; it is a testament to the love, grace, and unwavering support I have received from each of you. I am eternally grateful.

Why This Guide? Personal Story/Experience

This guide was born from a place of deep, aching loss and a fierce, unwavering love. I lost my husband and my mother within a span of two months. While the world around me carried on, my world felt as though it had come to a screeching halt. Yet, life didn't wait for me to grieve. My son, who has special needs, still needed me — to be present, to be strong, to be the mother he knew.

Grief became a silent companion, lingering in the corners of every room, in the spaces where my loved ones once existed. It was in the empty chair at the dinner table, in the phone that didn't ring, in the songs my mother used to hum while cooking. And yet, amidst that heartache, there was my son — a child whose needs didn't pause for my pain.

I wrote this guide for those who find themselves in this dual journey. For the parents who are grieving the loss of a loved one while tending to the needs of a child who relies on them, day in and day out. For the mothers who are holding it all together while falling apart inside. For the fathers who are aching to collapse but must stay strong for their children.

Navigating Grief

This is for you. To remind you that it's okay to grieve and to love, to break down and to rebuild, to honor the past and to keep moving forward. You are not alone in this. Let's walk this path together.

My Breaking Point

It was a Sunday like any other. The air was thick with the scent of freshly brewed tea, and the warm Florida sun filtered softly through the blinds. We were still in bed, playfully debating who would make the morning tea. That morning, I decided to pamper him. I brought a steaming cup to his bedside—unaware that it would be the last cup I'd ever make for him.

An hour later, he stepped out into the courtyard to trim the overgrown plants. It was such a mundane moment—ordinary, routine. Moments later, he returned inside, pale and breathless. "I feel tired," he said. He lay down and checked his heart rate on his smartwatch. The numbers flickered erratically—jumping from 40 to 150. That had never happened before.

He had no known health conditions. No warnings. I didn't hesitate. I called 911.

Those few minutes stretched endlessly. Paramedics rushed into our living room. I watched in helpless silence as they worked on him, then rushed him to the hospital. Within hours, he was gone. A massive heart attack had taken away the man I built my life with. Just like that.

The days that followed dissolved into a blur. Condolences. Casseroles. Kind words that could not touch the hollow ache inside. Friends and family flowed in and out of our home, arms filled with food, flowers, and prayers. Their love was real—but it couldn't reach the part of me that had just shattered. I was a shell. Screaming inside. Numb outside. Not crying. Almost functioning—at least for the world.

But the real storm was in my son's eyes.

Izyan. My little boy. Non-verbal. Limited vocabulary. Too innocent to grasp the weight of the word *death*. His father was no longer there to carry him on his shoulders, to take him swimming, to kiss him goodnight. And all he could say, over and over, in his own sweet way, was just one word: "Papa?"

That was the breaking point.

Not just the day I lost my husband. It was the day I lost my normal. The future we had planned. The stability I had relied on. The familiar rhythm of our home. Everything changed. Permanently.

Navigating Grief

Life, I've come to realize, is both cruelly brief and achingly beautiful.

You don't survive the breaking point by conquering it. You survive by breathing through it. By standing in the wreckage and whispering, "One more breath. One more step."

And slowly, with time, that breath becomes a heartbeat. That step becomes a path.

Grief and Grace

"Every scar holds a story, but the real power lies in how we use those stories to pave a path forward. Transform your pain into purpose — one step, one lesson, one practical action at a time."

How to Use This Guide: A Practical Approach

This guide is designed to be both a comforting companion and a practical toolkit. It is structured to provide actionable steps, reflective prompts, and personal exercises that can be integrated into your daily routine. Here's how you can make the most of it:

1. Read at Your Own Pace:
    - Grief doesn't follow a schedule, and neither should you. Take your time with each section. Pause, reflect, and revisit as needed.
2. Journal as You Go:
    - Throughout the guide, you will find reflective prompts. Keep a journal close by to write down your thoughts, feelings, and personal insights. These exercises are intended to help you process your emotions and track your healing journey.
3. Implement Small, Manageable Steps:
    - Each chapter includes practical exercises or suggestions. Focus on one action step at a time.

Grief and Grace

    Small, consistent actions can create meaningful shifts in your daily life.

4. Revisit Sections as Needed:
   - Grief is not linear. If a particular chapter resonates deeply or if a certain exercise feels right, don't hesitate to return to it whenever necessary.
5. Connect with Your Support Network:
   - Share sections or exercises with trusted friends, family members, or a therapist. Sometimes, discussing your reflections can offer additional insights and comfort.
6. Be Gentle with Yourself:
   - This guide is not about fixing grief; it's about holding space for it. Allow yourself to feel without judgment. Healing takes time, and every step, no matter how small, is progress.

Take a deep breath. Let's move forward together.

Navigating Grief While Raising a Special Needs Child

Introduction

Acknowledging the Dual Journey: Grieving a Loss While Caring for a Special Needs Child

> *"Life's most profound lessons are often wrapped in the unexpected. The journey may be unplanned, but the growth is inevitable." — Unknown*

I still remember the day everything shifted — the day the ground beneath my feet felt like it was crumbling. My son was three years old when the diagnosis came. Those words hung heavy in the air, and in that moment, life as I knew it split into two — the life I had imagined and the one I now faced.

Seven years later, just as I was finding my footing in the world of special needs parenting, life delivered another blow. My husband, my rock, was gone. My son was almost ten years old, and the weight of raising him alone pressed down on me like a dark, suffocating cloud.

Grief doesn't announce itself. It arrives quietly, in the moments when the house is too silent, the bed too empty, and the future too uncertain. But amid the heartache, something began to stir.

Grief and Grace

My son's laughter — the same laughter that echoed through the house when he was a toddler — became a balm for my aching heart. His resilience in the face of struggles I could barely comprehend became my guide, reminding me that even in the darkest chapters, there is still light.

This book isn't just a recounting of what was lost. It's a testament to what can still be found. It's about navigating grief while raising a child with special needs — not with perfection, but with grace, faith, and a steady, stubborn hope.

If you're holding this book, you are not alone. There is a way through the storm, and together, we will find it — one step, one day, one small moment of grace at a time.

Grief is never a straightforward path, but when you're navigating the deep waters of loss while simultaneously caring for a special needs child, the journey can feel impossibly heavy. You're caught between two worlds — mourning what you've lost and fiercely holding onto what remains. Every day becomes a balancing act of meeting your child's needs while tending to the aching void left by a loved one's absence.

This guide is here to walk you through this dual journey — not as a prescription for healing but as a compassionate companion to hold space for your grief and your responsibilities. You are not alone in this. There are others walking a similar path, and together, we will explore ways to honor your loss while embracing the present and finding renewed purpose in the life you are still living.

In the pages that follow, you will find practical steps, reflective prompts, and compassionate guidance designed to help you navigate grief without losing yourself, to honor the person you've lost without neglecting the person you're still becoming, and to care for your child while caring for your own heart too.

Let's begin!

Chapter 1: Understanding Grief

Defining Grief: Beyond Death

Grief is often associated with death, but it extends far beyond that. It's the emotional response to any form of loss — the loss of a loved one, the loss of a relationship, the loss of a way of life, or even the loss of the future you had envisioned.

For parents of special needs children, grief can be a recurring experience. It can arise not only from the death of a loved one but also from the realization that certain dreams, milestones, or expectations may not unfold as anticipated.

The Unique Grief of Parents of Special Needs Children

For parents of special needs children, grief can be a silent, unacknowledged experience. It's the unspoken sadness that comes when your child missed a milestones others take for granted. It's the ache of watching other children do what your child struggles to accomplish. It's the fear of the future and the worry about what will happen to your child when you're no longer around to care for them.

Navigating Grief

Grief in this context is complex because it's not just about loss — it's about continuous adjustment. Every medical appointment, every missed milestone, every unexpected diagnosis can bring a fresh wave of grief. And yet, you continue to show up, to parent, to love, and to nurture.

Common Emotions: Guilt, Anger, Isolation—and Why They're All Valid

When grief and special needs parenting intersect, emotions can become particularly intense and complex. Recognizing these feelings as normal responses to abnormal circumstances is an essential step toward processing them:

Guilt:
Guilt, manifests in numerous forms for grieving special needs parents:

- Caregiving guilt: "I'm not doing enough for my child because I'm overwhelmed by grief."
- Grieving guilt: "I don't have the right to fall apart when my child needs me."
- Survivor guilt: "Why am I here when they're gone?"
- Relief guilt: If your loved one suffered before death, feeling relief that their suffering has ended—which can conflict with your grief.

- Comparative guilt: "Others have it worse than me; I shouldn't feel this bad."

Anger:

Anger, may target:

- The person who died ("How could you leave us in this situation?")
- The medical system that failed to save them
- God or the universe for the unfairness of your situation
- Well-meaning people who offer unhelpful advice
- Yourself for struggles to cope

Anger is a natural response to injustice, and few things feel more unjust than navigating profound loss while caring for a child with special needs.

Isolation:

Isolation, in this context goes beyond just feeling lonely:

- Social isolation: Friends may withdraw because they don't know how to support both your grief and your child's needs.
- Emotional isolation: Feeling that no one truly understands your unique situation.

- Practical isolation: Being unable to attend support groups or social events due to caregiving responsibilities.
- Identity isolation: Feeling separate from both typical parents and typical grieving people.

Fear:

Fear, takes many forms:

- Fear about your ability to continue caregiving alone
- Fear about your child's future without their other parent or support person
- Fear about your own health and mortality
- Fear about financial security
- Fear that grief will never ease

Exhaustion:

Both grief and special needs parenting are energy-intensive. Together, they can create profound fatigue that affects:

- Physical stamina
- Emotional resilience
- Cognitive functioning (decision-making, memory, focus)
- Spiritual wellbeing

Unexpected Emotions

Many parents are surprised by emotions they didn't anticipate:

- Resentment toward the person who died
- Envy
- Numbness when you expected to feel sadness
- Relief from certain responsibilities
- Gratitude alongside grief

It's important to remember that these emotions are not wrong. They are valid responses to extraordinary circumstances. Giving yourself permission to feel them without judgment is a vital step toward healing.

The Myth of 'Moving On' vs. Moving Forward

There is a cultural pressure to "move on" after loss, but for parents of special needs children, the concept of moving on can feel impossible. How do you move on when you are still very much in the midst of caregiving? Instead, consider the concept of "moving forward." Moving forward doesn't mean leaving the grief behind. It means carrying it with you, integrating it into your life, and finding ways to continue living and loving despite it.

Navigating Grief
Reflection Prompts: Identifying Your Grief Triggers

- What are the moments when you feel the most profound sense of loss?
- Are there specific events or dates that amplify your grief?
- How do you respond when grief surfaces unexpectedly?
- What activities, people, or places tend to bring your grief to the surface?
- How can you create space to acknowledge and honor these feelings without feeling overwhelmed?

Take a moment to write down your reflections in next few pages. Allow yourself to feel without judgment.

Reflections

Navigating Grief

Reflections

Finding Me Again

Grief has a way of erasing everything you once knew — including yourself. The life you once lived, the roles you once played, the person you once were — all feel distant, almost unrecognizable. You find yourself moving through each day like a ghost, a hollow version of who you used to be. But in the depths of that emptiness, there is a chance to rebuild, to find yourself anew.

For a long time, I didn't know who I was anymore. Was I still a wife if my husband was gone? Was I still a daughter if my mother was no longer there to call? Somewhere in the silence that grief left behind, a small, stubborn part of me refused to disappear. Maybe it was the echo of my mother's voice, reminding me that I was still here, that I still mattered. Maybe it was the sight of my son, his little face looking up at me with eyes so much like his father's. Maybe it was the simple fact that I was still breathing, still waking up every morning, still surviving.

Slowly, I started to rebuild myself — not the woman I once was, but someone new, someone forged in fire and loss. I began to say "yes" to things I would have once declined. An invitation to coffee with a colleague. A weekend art class. A walk around the park at sunset.

Each "yes" was a step forward, a small act of reclaiming my life. I wasn't healed, but I was beginning to live again. It was a slow process, one that required patience, acceptance, and a willingness to let go of the life I thought I would always have.

The process of finding myself again wasn't about forgetting the past or erasing the pain. It was about integrating those losses into the new person I was becoming — a woman who had loved deeply and lost deeply but was still standing, still growing, still becoming.

Finding yourself again after profound loss is not about becoming who you once were. It's about allowing yourself to become who you're meant to be now — someone who can hold both love and loss, both joy and grief, both the memories of what was and the possibilities of what still can be. And in that space, between what is gone and what remains, you may just find the person you were always meant to become.

Grief and Grace
Milestones and Memory Markers

There are certain days that amplify the echoes of loss—birthdays, anniversaries, and other significant dates. They act as reminders of the life we once had and the life, we continue to navigate without those we love. Below blog post I wrote in my journal in one of those dates,

"Today, as Izyan celebrates his 16th birthday, my heart is a swirling storm of emotions. The day brings with it a wave of nostalgia, a deep ache of longing for Sharique, and a bittersweet sense of pride as I reflect on the journey we have traveled.

I remember the day Izyan was born as vividly as if it were yesterday. I was younger, happily married, and eagerly awaiting the arrival of our precious baby. That early morning rush to the hospital, the anticipation, the pain, the overwhelming joy as Izyan entered the world at 1 pm—it was a moment etched in my memory as one of the most beautiful days of my life.

Life back then felt perfect, almost dreamlike in its blissful simplicity. But life had its own plans. Parenthood came with its own set of challenges—the sleepless nights, the endless diaper changes, the uncertainty of raising a child. Yet, even amidst the

Navigating Grief

exhaustion, the joy of those early years remains vivid, overshadowing the struggles.

Izyan, my sweet boy, captured my heart instantly and has continued to be my world. The unexpected twist in our story came when he was diagnosed with autism at the age of three. I grieved the future I had envisioned for him, a future that now seemed uncertain and unfamiliar. The diagnosis was a heavy blow, a reminder that life doesn't always go as planned. But it also became a turning point in how I approached motherhood.

I made a vow to myself—to embrace Izyan for who he is, to nurture the best version of him, to love him fiercely without the weight of expectations. Today, as Izyan turns 16, I can't help but reflect on how far we've come. Our journey has diverged from the typical teenage milestones. While his peers navigate high school, social life, and driving lessons, Izyan remains the innocent boy who finds joy in simple activities—playing in the park, and watching his favorite cartoons. There are days when I feel like I've fallen short as a mother, days when I question whether I'm enough. But then, there are moments when I look at Izyan and see how far we've both come. Those are the moments that remind me that while our path may be different, it is uniquely ours.

Grief and Grace

As I sip my tea and reflect on this milestone birthday, I am overwhelmed with gratitude for the privilege of being Izyan's mother. His path may not be conventional, but it is filled with its own beauty—a beauty I am honored to witness and nurture every single day. In embracing his journey, I am also embracing my own, one day at a time, with love, acceptance, and grace."

Chapter 2: The Overlap of Grief and Parenting

Emotional Exhaustion: The Double Burden

"Parenting a special needs child isn't about fixing; it's about embracing. It's not about making them like everyone else; it's about helping them thrive as they are." — *unknown*

Parenting is already a demanding role. Add grief to the equation, and the emotional weight can feel nearly unbearable. You're expected to be present, nurturing, and attentive while also carrying the invisible weight of your own heartache.

Grief drains your energy, clouds your mind, and heightens your emotions. Parenting requires focus, patience, and empathy — qualities that grief often consumes. It's not uncommon to feel

Grief and Grace

like you're failing at both, unable to give either the attention they demand. This double burden can lead to burnout, emotional numbness, or a sense of being pulled in too many directions at once.

Acceptance is the first step toward finding peace as a parent. When you stop trying to fix your child or comparing them to others, you open yourself up to a more profound, more fulfilling connection. The truth is, as long as you focus on what your child cannot do, you will remain in a constant state of frustration, exhaustion, and grief. But the moment you shift your focus to what they can do, to the unique qualities that make them who they are, that is the moment everything changes.

Comparison is a thief of joy. It is an insidious cycle that robs you of the present moment, pulling you into a spiral of 'what ifs' and 'why nots.' But the fact that your child is here, in your life, giving you the chance to experience parenthood — that is a blessing in itself. There are countless people who yearn for that very opportunity, a chance to be a 'Mom' or 'Dad,' to hold a tiny hand, to share the small, quiet moments that often go unnoticed.

The reality is, there will always be someone with a smarter child or an easier parenting journey. But comparing to that will only drain you of the energy you need to nurture the unique bond you share with your child. Instead of asking why your child is not like others, start asking how you can celebrate who they already are. Celebrate the small victories, the baby steps that might seem insignificant to others but are monumental for you and your child.

Life isn't about checking off milestones on a societal checklist; it's about cherishing the journey as it unfolds, in all its unpredictable, beautiful messiness. Your child may not follow the typical path, but their path is no less valuable. When you learn to accept them without conditions, you begin to accept yourself as well. And in that acceptance, peace becomes possible.

Acknowledge the Exhaustion:

- Accept that it's okay to feel tired, overwhelmed, or even resentful. You are not failing; you are human.
- Allow yourself moments of rest without guilt. A 10-minute nap, a walk outside, or a few deep breaths can serve as micro-recharges throughout the day.

Balancing Self-Care with Child Care

Self-care feels like a luxury when you're grieving and parenting. But it's not a luxury — it's a necessity. The challenge is finding time and space for it without feeling like you're neglecting your child.

Practical Self-Care Strategies:

- **Micro Moments of Self-Care:** Instead of waiting for an hour-long break that may never come, focus on small, intentional acts: a cup of tea, a few minutes of deep breathing, or simply sitting in silence.
- **Boundary Setting:** It's okay to say no to things that drain you, even if they seem important. Protect your energy by setting limits on social interactions or tasks that feel overwhelming

- **Routine Resets:** Incorporate one small self-care activity into your daily routine. This could be as simple as journaling for five minutes before bed or listening to calming music while preparing meals.

Understanding Your Child's Emotional Needs

Children, especially those with special needs, may express their emotions in ways that are difficult to interpret. They may act out, withdraw, or become unusually clingy. Recognizing their grief is essential, even if they don't fully understand it.

Strategies to Support Your Child:

- **Consistent Communication:** Keep communication open, even if your child is non-verbal or struggles to express emotions. Use simple, reassuring language like, "I know things feel different. It's okay to feel sad or confused."
- **Predictability and Routine:** Grief can make life feel unpredictable. Maintaining a predictable daily routine can provide a sense of stability and security for your child.
- **Safe Spaces for Expression:** Encourage your child to express their feelings through art, music, or sensory

activities. Sometimes, emotions come out more easily through play than through words.

Finding Routine in Chaos: Practical Strategies

Grief disrupts routines. Days blur together, and even the simplest tasks can feel insurmountable. Creating small pockets of structure can provide a sense of normalcy amidst the chaos.

Daily Routine Strategies:

- **Anchor Activities:** Identify 2-3 key activities that anchor your day, such as morning tea, a daily walk, or bedtime reading. These become predictable moments that ground you and your child.
- **Visual Schedules:** Create a simple, visual schedule that outlines the day's activities. This can be especially helpful for children who thrive on routine.
- **Task Chunking:** Break tasks into smaller steps. Instead of "clean the house," focus on "fold the laundry" or "wipe down the kitchen counter." This makes tasks feel more manageable.

Navigating Grief
Exercise: Creating a Daily Grief and Care Journal

A daily journal can serve as both a grief outlet and a tool for managing parenting tasks. Here's how to structure it:

Section 1: Emotional Check-In reflections in next page

_____
_____
_____
_____
_____
_____
_____
_____
_____
_____
_____
_____
_____
_____
_____
_____
_____
_____
_____

Grief and Grace

How am I feeling today

Reflections

Navigating Grief
What triggered my grief today?

Reflections

Grief and Grace
What small moment brought me comfort or joy?

Reflections

Section 2: Child Care Priorities

What does my child need most today?

_____
_____
_____
_____
_____
_____
_____
_____
_____

How can I support them emotionally today?

_____
_____
_____
_____
_____
_____
_____
_____
_____

Section 3: Self-Care Goals

What can I do for myself today, even if it's just for 5 minutes?

_____
_____
_____
_____
_____
_____
_____
_____
_____

What boundary can I set to protect my energy?

_____
_____
_____
_____
_____
_____
_____
_____
_____

How can I be gentle with myself today?

_____
_____
_____
_____
_____
_____
_____
_____
_____

Section 4: Gratitude and Reflection

One thing I am grateful for today.

_____
_____
_____
_____
_____
_____
_____
_____
_____
_____

Grief and Grace

A small win or accomplishment.

_____
_____
_____
_____
_____
_____
_____
_____
_____

A kind word or affirmation to carry me through the day.

_____
_____
_____
_____
_____
_____
_____
_____
_____

Chapter 3: Embracing Support Systems

"It's okay to ask for help. It's okay to lean on others. We weren't meant to walk this road alone." — *Unknown*

Identifying Support Systems: Friends, Family, Therapists

Grief can feel isolating, but you don't have to carry it alone. Identifying your support system is crucial. Start by listing people in your life who can provide emotional, practical, or logistical support. This may include close friends, family members, and therapists.

Finding Specialized Support Groups for Special Needs Families

There are specific support groups for parents of special needs children who are also grieving. These groups offer a safe space to share experiences, connect with others who understand, and receive guidance from those further along the path.

Grief and Grace
Building a Personal Support Network

Your network doesn't have to be large; it just has to be reliable. Consider reaching out to:

- Family members who can help with caregiving.
- Friends who can provide emotional support or practical help.
- Therapists specializing in grief and special needs parenting.
- Online communities or local support groups.

Asking for Help Without Guilt

Asking for help isn't a sign of weakness; it's a sign of wisdom. Be specific about what you need. Instead of saying, "I need help," try, "Can you pick up groceries for me this week?" or "Could you watch my child for an hour while I take a walk?"

Who Is Your Support System?

_____
_____
_____
_____
_____
_____
_____

Navigating Grief

Who can you call on during difficult days?

_____
_____
_____
_____
_____
_____
_____
_____

What specific tasks or responsibilities can you delegate?

_____
_____
_____
_____
_____
_____
_____
_____

Grief and Grace

How can you express gratitude to those who show up for you?

_____
_____
_____
_____
_____
_____
_____
_____

Are there new connections you could make, such as joining a support group or reaching out to a local therapist?

_____
_____
_____
_____
_____
_____
_____
_____

Navigating Grief

Take some time to write down your reflections. Recognize that support is a two-way street — allowing others to help can also be a gift to them.

HEALTHY COPING SKILLS

Read	Self-care	Have fun	Meditate
Music	Take a break	Pet an animal	Breathe
Laugh	Cook or bake	Go outside	Vent
Create	Clean	Rest	Exercise

Navigating Grief

"Grief is not the end of the story; it's the ink that rewrites the chapters you never saw coming."

Chapter 4: Finding Purpose Amidst Loss

The Sacredness of the Ordinary

Life has a way of shifting without warning. One moment everything feels familiar and routine—your morning coffee, the school run, a shared dinner at the end of a long day. And then, in the blink of an eye, that normalcy can become a memory too painful to revisit or too precious to hold without tears. What we often see as mundane is, in truth, sacred.

> *We go through life assuming we have time. We assume the people we love will always be around. We sit across from them at dinner tables, lie beside them in bed, share quiet moments in the car or loud ones in the kitchen, and yet—our minds are elsewhere. On our phones, in our to-do lists, lost in distraction. We think we'll always have another day to say, "I love you," "I'm sorry," or simply, "Tell me how your day was." But we don't.*

The harsh and humbling truth is this: every relationship we have is a loan from God. No one—no matter how much we love them—is ours to keep. Every person who walks through our life is a temporary gift. And we don't get to choose when that gift is

Navigating Grief

taken back. We don't know when the last conversation will be. The last shared meal. The last time you'll hear their voice or feel their touch. There is always a last time, and we almost never see it coming.

That is why we must live with reverence for the now.

Treasure the people around you. Put the phone down. Look into their eyes. Laugh with them. Be present. Not just physically, but emotionally and spiritually. Say what needs to be said. Hug a little longer. Forgive a little quicker. Appreciate a little deeper. Prioritize people over perfection. Don't let the laundry or the emails steal moments you'll one day ache for.

Even the messes of life are blessings in disguise. A sink full of dishes means you had food to eat. Toys scattered on the floor mean children's laughter echoed through the house. A cluttered schedule means you have purpose and responsibility—things others may be praying for. The noise, the chaos, the exhaustion—it all points to a life that is alive, a life that is full.

So, pause. Take a deep breath. Look around.

Right now—this very moment—is someone else's answered prayer. Don't rush through it. Don't wait for something big to

Grief and Grace

happen to start appreciating the small things. Because one day, these will be the big things.

Romanticize your life. Let your life be one where people are cherished, time is honored, and love is never assumed but always expressed.

Navigating Grief
You are still alive!!

You are stronger than you realize.
Grief may have shaken the ground beneath you, but it did not break you. You are still here — showing up, holding on, and finding ways to keep moving forward.

In every tear shed, there is a story of love that refuses to be forgotten. In every moment of exhaustion, there is a reminder of how fiercely you continue to fight for your child and yourself. And in every day that you get up, despite the heaviness of loss, there is undeniable proof of your resilience.

You have navigated the unimaginable, carrying both the weight of grief and the responsibility of caregiving. That is no small feat. Let this be your reminder: You are not just surviving — you are rebuilding, transforming, and rising.

Your heart may feel heavy, but it is also a vessel of profound strength. Your days may feel uncertain, but you are finding ways to create stability. Your life may feel fragmented, but you are piecing it back together — one act of courage, one moment of grace, one step at a time.

You are more than your pain. You are more than your loss. You are a testament to the power of persistence, love, and faith.

Grief and Grace
Keep going. You are not alone.

Finding Calmness Through Living Memorials

When someone we love is no longer physically present, the world often urges us to "move on," as if the void can simply be filled or forgotten. But what if, instead of moving on, we chose to move forward — carrying their essence within us, not as a weight, but as a source of calm and quiet joy?

A living memorial is not about creating grand gestures or public displays. It's about the small, personal rituals that anchor you to their memory, not in grief but in gentle remembrance. Light a candle in the evening and let its warm glow remind you of the light they brought into your life. Cook their favorite meal and savor it, not in sorrow but in gratitude for the moments you shared. Hold onto a keepsake that once belonged to them, letting it ground you in the love that still lingers.

Because what's gone cannot come back, but the essence of who they were — the love, the lessons, the memories — can still find a home in your heart. Instead of seeking closure, let these moments of connection become a living, breathing memorial, a way to keep their presence alive in the everyday, not as a haunting but as a comforting reminder that love, in its purest form, never truly fades.

Ideas for Living Memorials:

- Start a journal where you write letters to them whenever you feel the need to connect.

- Dedicate a day each month to do something they loved — whether it's visiting their favorite café or playing their favorite song.

How to Honor the Memory of Your Loved One

Honoring the memory of a loved one is deeply personal. It can be as simple as speaking their name aloud or as involved as creating a community initiative in their name. The key is to choose actions that align with who they were and what they loved.

Grief and Grace

Ways to Honor Their Memory:

- **Acts of Service:** Volunteer for a cause they were passionate about or donate to a charity in their name.
- **Memory Boxes:** Collect items that remind you of them — photos, letters, mementos — and keep them in a special box to revisit when you need to feel close to them.
- **Annual Rituals:** Create a family tradition, such as a meal or a special outing, to remember them each year on their birthday or anniversary.

Lessons in Resilience: Reframing Pain as Strength

When the ground beneath you crumbles and the life you once knew shatters, it's natural to feel paralyzed by the weight of loss. The absence of a loved one can leave you feeling untethered, as if the world has shifted and you're left standing in the aftermath, wondering how to take the next step.

But what if this pain, as unbearable as it feels, is also the very thing that can transform you? What if, instead of burying it, you allowed yourself to feel it — fully, deeply, honestly?

Resilience isn't about pretending you're okay or ignoring the ache. It's about sitting with it, letting the tears flow, and gradually rebuilding a new foundation, one stone at a time. You don't have to rush it. Let the pain teach you about your strength, about the depths of your heart, about the capacity you have to endure.

Because while the loss may have taken a part of you, it has also revealed a part you never knew existed — the part that can still stand, still breathe, still find a way forward, even when everything feels broken.

Reframing Techniques:

- **From 'Why Me?' to 'What Now?':** Instead of asking why this happened, consider how you can channel your grief into something meaningful — whether it's helping others, creating art, or simply showing up for yourself and your child each day.

- **Trusting God and His Plan:** In moments of deep pain, it can be difficult to understand why certain things happen. Leaning into faith can provide a source of comfort and strength. Remind yourself that while you may not see the entire picture, God's plan is always at work, even amidst the heartache. Trust that there is purpose in your pain, even if it's not yet visible.

- **From 'I'll Never Be the Same' to 'I Am Evolving':** Loss changes us. It forces us to redefine who we are without the person we lost. Instead of resisting this change, lean into it and ask yourself, "What strengths have I discovered in myself through this process?" Embrace the idea that God is guiding you through a journey of growth and transformation.

Creating New Traditions with Your Child

When life as you once knew it feels like a distant memory, grief can cast a shadow over even the simplest routines. The emptiness left behind can feel all-consuming, as though every day is a reminder of what was lost. But amid the ache, there is a way to reclaim a sense of continuity — by creating new traditions with your child.

Think about the small, simple acts that can anchor you both — a Sunday morning walk, a special dinner once a month, a bedtime ritual that offers comfort. These moments may not erase the loss, but they can weave new threads of connection, reminding you that while the past cannot return, the present still holds room for love, laughter, and moments of quiet joy.

New traditions don't have to be elaborate or perfect. They just need to be yours — little pockets of consistency that remind your child (and yourself) that life, though different, can still hold meaning, warmth, and moments of shared tenderness.

Ideas for New Traditions:

- **Memory Walks:** Take regular walks with your child and talk about their loved one. Share stories, look for signs of nature that remind you of them, or simply enjoy the quiet togetherness.
- **Gratitude Rituals:** Each evening, share one thing you're grateful for. This practice not only fosters connection but also helps to cultivate a sense of grounding and presence.
- **Creative Projects:** Work on a scrapbook or memory board together, filled with photos, drawings, or written memories of your loved one. It can become a tangible reminder of their ongoing presence in your lives.

Exercise: Write a Letter to Your Lost Loved One

Writing is a powerful outlet, writing a letter to your loved one can be a powerful way to process grief and stay connected to their memory. Set aside some quiet time, find a comfortable space, and allow yourself to write freely.

Prompts for the Letter:

- What do you miss the most about them?
- What would you say to them if they were sitting across from you right now?
- What are some moments you wish they could be here to witness or experience?
- What do you want them to know about how you and your child are doing?
- How has their memory continued to impact your life?

You can choose to keep this letter in a special place, revisit it later, or even write additional letters whenever you feel the need. *It's not about finding closure but about creating an ongoing dialogue with the person you love.*

Chapter 5: Mindfulness and Emotional Regulation

"When life shakes you to your core, faith is the anchor that keeps you grounded." — *Unknown*

Simple Techniques to Stay Grounded

Grief can feel like a relentless storm, tossing you around with no sense of direction, leaving you disoriented and unsteady. On some days, it feels as if the ground beneath you is constantly shifting, and finding a moment of calm seems impossible.

But in those moments when everything feels too heavy, there are small, intentional ways to anchor yourself — to bring your mind back to the present and remind yourself that even amidst the chaos, there is still a place of calm within you.

Try placing your feet firmly on the ground and taking a few deep breaths, feeling the connection between you and the earth beneath you. Hold onto a comforting object — a smooth stone, a piece of fabric, or a keepsake that belonged to your loved one — and let its texture remind you that you are still here, still breathing, still capable of finding moments of stillness.

Grief and Grace

Grief may pull you in every direction, but grounding techniques can gently bring you back to yourself, to this moment, to the steady rhythm of your own heartbeat. And in that stillness, you might just find a sliver of calm.

Techniques to Stay Grounded:

5-4-3-2-1 Technique:

- Name 5 things you can see
- 4 things you can touch
- 3 things you can hear
- 2 things you can smell
- 1 thing you can taste

  This technique helps to bring your focus back to the present moment and out of the whirlpool of grief.

Mindful Parenting Practices

Parenting through grief requires you to be present for your child while also managing your own emotional turmoil. Mindful parenting can help you stay connected to your child while also taking care of yourself.

Navigating Grief

Mindful Parenting Practices:

- **Embrace Imperfection:**

You don't need to be the perfect parent right now. Show up as you are. Let your child see your humanity. This can teach them that it's okay to feel big emotions and still be okay.

- **Pause and Breathe:**

Before responding to a tantrum or emotional outburst, take three deep breaths. This moment of pause can help you respond with intention rather than react out of frustration.

- **Present Moment Check-Ins:**

Take five minutes to sit with your child and simply observe. Watch them play, draw, or talk without intervening. This practice fosters connection and reminds you both that you are still here, together, in this moment.

Grief and Grace
Breathing Exercises for Stress Relief

Breathing exercises are simple yet powerful tools to calm the mind and body. When grief feels heavy or overwhelming, these exercises can help release tension and bring a sense of calm. My friend, Neel, who got me introduced to yoga and meditation, urged me to practice below techniques.

Breathing Techniques:

- **4-7-8 Breathing:**
- Inhale through your nose for a count of 4
- Hold your breath for a count of 7
- Exhale slowly through your mouth for a count of 8
  Repeat this cycle three times. This technique helps to calm the nervous system and reduce anxiety.
- **Reflection Breathing:**
- Inhale for 4 counts
- Hold for 4 counts
- Exhale for 4 counts
- Hold for 4 counts
  Repeat for 5-7 cycles. This technique is particularly effective for grounding and centering.

Guided Visualization: Safe Space for Grieving

Visualization can create a mental sanctuary where you can release emotions and feel comforted. This practice allows you to visit a place in your mind where you feel safe, secure, and connected.

Guided Visualization Exercise:

- Find a quiet, comfortable space where you won't be disturbed. Close your eyes and take three slow, deep breaths.
- Imagine yourself in a place that brings you peace — it could be a beach, a garden, a cozy room, or a familiar childhood spot.
- Notice the details: What do you see? Hear? Feel? Smell?
- Imagine a warm, comforting presence by your side — it could be your loved one, a spiritual guide, or even your own compassionate self.
- Allow yourself to speak or listen to this presence. Let whatever needs to be said or heard flow naturally.
- When you're ready, take a deep breath and slowly bring your awareness back to the present moment. Open your eyes and take a few more grounding breaths.

Exercise: Daily Gratitude Practice

Gratitude may seem impossible in the midst of grief, but even the smallest moments of appreciation can provide a lifeline during difficult days.

Daily Gratitude Practice:

- At the end of each day, write down three things you are grateful for. They don't have to be big or profound — they could be as simple as a warm cup of tea, a kind word from a friend, or a moment of quiet.
- Reflect on why each item brought you comfort or relief. This practice helps shift your focus from what is missing to what is still present and good in your life.
- Over time, revisit these entries. Notice the small pockets of light that have sustained you even in the darkest moments.

Navigating Grief

Reflections

Grief and Grace

Reflections

Chapter 6: Navigating Uncertainty and Future Planning

Planning for Your Child's Future in the Absence of a Partner

The thought of not being there for your child one day can feel overwhelming. For parents of special needs children, this concern is often magnified. Who will care for them? Will they be safe, supported, and loved? Planning for your child's future in the absence of a partner is not only a practical step but also a compassionate one — for both you and your child.

Steps to Consider:

- **Identify Potential Guardians:**

Choose someone you trust, someone who understands your child's needs and is willing to take on this role. This could be a family member, a close friend, or even a trusted caregiver.

- **Communicate Your Wishes:**

Have open, honest conversations with potential guardians. Share your child's daily routine, medical needs, educational plans, and emotional triggers. Document these in a comprehensive guide that they can refer to if needed.

- **Create a Support Network:**

Don't rely on a single person. Create a network of trusted individuals — family, therapists, community members — who can step in to provide support if needed

- **Establish Legal Arrangements:**

Work with a legal advisor to formalize guardianship plans. This ensures your wishes are legally binding and reduces potential conflicts.

Financial Considerations: Trusts, Funds, and Resources

Financial planning is critical to ensuring your child's future stability. Setting up the right financial structures can alleviate worry and provide ongoing support, even in your absence.

Options to Consider:

- **Special Needs Trust:**

A special needs trust can provide financial support for your child without jeopardizing their eligibility for government assistance. This trust is managed by a trustee who allocates funds according to your instructions.

- **Savings and Investment Accounts:**

Set up savings accounts designated for your child's future care. Consider conservative investments that offer steady returns over time.

- **Life Insurance Policies:**

Consider a life insurance policy with your child as the beneficiary. This can provide financial security in the event of your passing.

- **Government Resources and Programs:**

Research available state and federal programs that provide financial support, healthcare, and housing assistance for special needs individuals.

Creating a Legacy Plan: Documenting Your Wishes

A legacy plan ensures that your wishes are clearly outlined and accessible to those who will care for your child after you're gone. This plan is not only about financial arrangements but also about preserving your values, hopes, and intentions.

Components of a Legacy Plan:

- **Letter of Intent:**

Write a letter to your child's future caregiver(s) that details your child's routine, medical needs, preferences, fears, and comforting practices. Include contact information for trusted professionals (therapists, doctors, teachers).

- **Emotional Legacy:**

Include messages of love, encouragement, and life advice for your child. This could be in the form of letters, videos, or journals.

- **Personal Values and Traditions:**

Document traditions you'd like to see continued. Whether it's a specific birthday ritual, a religious practice, or simply how you celebrate holidays, these small acts of continuity can provide your child with a sense of stability and connection.

- **Guidelines for Care:**

Clearly outline expectations for your child's care. Include information about therapy schedules, medication routines, dietary preferences, and educational plans.

Reflection Prompts: What Does a Secure Future Look Like?

Take a moment to reflect on the following prompts:

- What are the three most important things you want for your child in the future?

_____
_____
_____
_____
_____
_____
_____
_____
_____
_____
_____
_____
_____
_____
_____
_____
_____

Grief and Grace

- Who in your circle do you trust to uphold your values and care for your child in your absence?

  _____
  _____
  _____
  _____
  _____
  _____
  _____
  _____
  _____
  _____

- How do you feel about documenting your wishes? What is holding you back from doing so?

  _____
  _____
  _____
  _____
  _____
  _____
  _____
  _____
  _____
  _____

Navigating Grief

- What financial steps can you take today to provide long-term security for your child?

- If you could leave one message or piece of advice for your child to read when they are older, what would it be?

Grief and Grace

Write down your responses. Allow yourself to feel whatever comes up without judgment. This exercise is not about finding immediate solutions but about clarifying your intentions and identifying the next steps.

Chapter 7: Finding Meaning and Rebuilding Identity

Reconnecting with Passions and Purpose

"Resilience isn't about bouncing back; it's about growing through what you go through." — *Unknown*

Grief has a way of consuming every aspect of life, leaving us feeling untethered and directionless. Reconnecting with passions and rediscovering purpose can serve as a lifeline, a way to reclaim a sense of self amidst the loss.

Steps to Reconnect with Your Passions:

- **Recall What Used to Light You Up:**

  Make a list of activities you once loved but abandoned. Did you love painting? Writing? Gardening? Spending time in nature? Choose one and reintroduce it, even in a small way.

- **Create Space for Curiosity:**

Grief can make it feel as though life is on hold. But taking even 10 minutes a day to explore a hobby or interest can reignite a spark of aliveness.

- **Combine Passion with Purpose:**

If you loved writing, consider journaling about your grief journey or sharing your story in a blog. If you enjoyed cooking, host a dinner for other grieving parents. Sometimes, passions can evolve to reflect where we are now.

Turning Pain into Purpose: Community Outreach or Volunteering

When life feels fractured, finding ways to help others can create a renewed sense of purpose. Giving back can also be a healing act, a way to honor your loved one while making a positive impact.

Ways to Turn Pain into Purpose:

- **Volunteer with Support Groups:**

Share your experience with those going through similar losses. Your story can provide comfort and a sense of connection.

- **Create a Memorial Fund:**

Start a small fund to support causes your loved one cared about — whether it's supporting special needs children, funding a scholarship, or contributing to grief support initiatives.

- **Organize a Community Event:**

Host a workshop, a walk, or a gathering in memory of your loved one. Use the opportunity to raise awareness, share resources, or simply bring people together.

- **Start a Blog or Support Group:**

Share your journey through grief and parenting, offering practical advice, emotional support, and hope to those navigating similar paths.

Journaling Prompts: Rewriting Your Story

Journaling can serve as a bridge between the person you were before the loss and the person you are becoming. It allows you to explore your evolving identity while processing complex emotions.

Journaling Prompts:

- What part of yourself do you feel you lost with your loved one?

- What qualities or strengths have emerged through this journey?

- How has grief reshaped your priorities or values?

Grief and Grace

- If your loved one could see you now, what would they say to you?

- What passions or interests have you discovered or rediscovered since the loss?

- In what ways can you honor your loved one through your actions and choices?

Navigating Grief

Grief and Grace

Navigating Grief

5 minute journaling

ONE THING I WANT TO REMEMBER ABOUT TODAY

___

___

___

___

___

TODAY I FELT...

___

___

___

___

___

TODAY I'M GREATFUL FOR

___

___

___

___

___

Exercise: Visualizing Your 'New Normal'

Grief creates a rupture in the life you once knew, leaving you to rebuild in its wake. This exercise will guide you through visualizing a new normal — a life where you can honor the past while embracing the present.

Exercise Steps:

1. **Find a Quiet Space:**

Sit comfortably and close your eyes. Take a few deep breaths, allowing yourself to settle.

2. **Visualize Your Ideal Day:**

Picture a day where you feel calm, grounded, and purposeful. What does this day look like? Where are you? What are you doing?

3. **Identify What Remains and What Has Changed:**

Notice what parts of your life still feel familiar and which parts are new or different.

4. **Imagine Your Loved One's Presence:**

In this new day, where is the memory of your loved one? Is it in a photo on the wall, a song on the radio, a piece of jewelry you wear.

5. **Reflect and Journal:**

Open your eyes and write down what you visualized. Include as many sensory details as possible. How did you feel during this exercise? What aspects of this new normal feel within reach?

_____
_____
_____
_____
_____
_____
_____
_____
_____
_____
_____
_____
_____
_____

Grief and Grace
Bringing God and Spirituality into Your Healing Journey

In the midst of loss, grief can feel like an endless void — a space where nothing makes sense and the future feels uncertain. But for many, faith can serve as a guiding light, a source of comfort and strength when the world feels too heavy to bear. Inviting God or a spiritual practice into your healing journey doesn't erase the pain, but it can provide a sense of purpose, perspective, and connection.

Finding Meaning in God's Plan

When tragedy strikes, it's natural to question, "Why did this happen?" or "Why did God allow this?" While these questions may not have clear answers, faith invites us to trust that there is a purpose beyond what we can see.

- **Surrendering to God's Will:**

Letting go doesn't mean forgetting your loved one or moving on without them. It means releasing the need to control the outcome and trusting that God's plan is unfolding as it should. Pray for the strength to accept what is, even when it feels unfair.

- **Seeking God's Presence in Small Moments:**

Grief can make you feel disconnected from everything, including God. Create intentional moments to reconnect — through prayer, reading scripture, or sitting quietly in nature. Invite God to sit with you in your sorrow, to carry some of the weight you're holding.

Turning Pain into Prayer

When words fail, prayer becomes a powerful outlet. You don't need eloquent language; speak from your heart. If you don't know what to say, consider these simple prayers:

- **Prayer for Strength:**

"God, I feel lost and overwhelmed. Give me the strength to get through today. Hold me close and remind me that I am not alone."

- **Prayer for Peace:**

"God, calm the storm inside me. Help me find moments of stillness amidst the chaos. Let Your peace fills the spaces where my heart is aching."

- **Prayer for Guidance:**

"God, I don't know what comes next. Guide me forward. Show me the path and give me the courage to walk it."

Grief and Grace
Finding God in Your Child's Eyes

Your child is a living, breathing reminder of love, resilience, and hope. When you feel disconnected from God, look at your child — the way they smile, the way they reach for you, the way they trust without hesitation.

- **Embrace the Innocence of Faith:**

Children often believe without question. Take a moment to pray with your child, even if it's as simple as saying, "Thank you, God, for this day." It doesn't have to be perfect; it just has to be honest.

- **Create Spiritual Rituals Together:**

Light a candle in memory of your loved one, say a prayer before meals, or read a comforting passage before bed. These small acts can become sacred rituals that ground you both in faith.

Spiritual Gratitude Practice

Grief can obscure the blessings still present in your life. A spiritual gratitude practice can help shift your focus from what is missing to what remains.

- **Daily Gratitude Prayer:**

At the end of each day, thank God for three things — a moment of connection, a small sign of your loved one's presence, the

Navigating Grief
strength to make it through another day.

Grief and Grace
Chapter 8: Romanticize Your Life

Grief rearranges everything. It strips life to its bones. But once the dust begins to settle—slowly, quietly—something remarkable begins to happen: you begin to see life differently. Sharper. Softer. Simpler. More sacred.

In the wake of profound loss, the question isn't how to return to your "old" life. The truth is, you don't. The question becomes: **how do you find beauty in this new one?** That's where the quiet revolution begins—when you decide to romanticize your life.

This doesn't mean living in denial. It means finding meaning in the mundane. It means honoring your pain *and* choosing to notice the glimmers that still exist all around you and to be authentic to yourself.

Light a candle for no reason. Take yourself on a walk without your phone. Make tea in your favorite cup, even when it's just you. Write letters you may never send. Play the song you love, dance in your kitchen. Make your bed with intention. Dress up to go nowhere. Pause to feel the breeze, notice how the sun warms your skin, or how rain sounds when it hits the roof.

Navigating Grief

These small acts are not indulgences—they are **reminders**: that you are still here. That joy, however quiet, still wants to sit beside your sorrow. That you are worthy of beauty, even in brokenness.

You don't need a perfect life to romanticize it. You just need to *see* it. Grief might have rewritten your story, but you still hold the pen. So, write beauty into the margins. Let your life become art again.

Let this be your new rhythm:
A life where mourning and magic coexist.
A life where healing doesn't wait for perfection.
A life where grace lives in everyday moments.

Because in the end, romanticizing your life is not about ignoring the pain—it's about choosing to see the poetry that quietly lingers, even in the shadows.

Conclusion: A Path Forward

Grief is not a destination; it's a journey — one that ebbs and flows, rises and falls, heals and breaks open again. You don't have to walk it perfectly, and you don't have to walk it alone.

In this guide, we've explored the dual journey of grieving while parenting a special needs child. We've acknowledged the heaviness of emotional exhaustion, the complexity of balancing self-care with childcare, and the importance of creating new routines amidst the chaos.

We've also delved into finding meaning and purpose, whether through living memorials, acts of service, or reconnecting with passions. And we've explored the profound role that faith and spirituality can play in grounding us, holding us, and reminding us that even in our darkest hours, we are not forsaken.

Now, as you close this book, take a moment to honor your own journey. You have faced days where the weight of loss felt insurmountable, and yet, here you are — still standing, still breathing, still moving forward. That is no small feat.

Navigating Grief

Before you go, here are some practical next steps:

1. Revisit the Exercises: Go back to the sections that resonated most with you. Spend time journaling, reflecting, and processing. Healing is not linear, and these exercises are here to support you whenever you need them.
2. Stay Connected: Reach out to trusted friends, family, or support groups. You are not meant to walk this path alone. Sharing your story can be both cathartic and a powerful source of connection.
3. Create a Ritual of Remembrance: Choose a small act — lighting a candle, writing a letter, or visiting a favorite place — that honors your loved one. These rituals can serve as grounding reminders of love that still lives on.
4. Take One Small Step Forward: Pick one action from the book that you feel ready to implement. Maybe it's starting a daily gratitude practice, reaching out to a support group, or taking a few minutes each morning to breathe deeply. Small steps matter.
5. Embrace the Present Moment: Yes, you have lost much, but there is still life to be lived, still love to be shared, still moments of grace to be found. Let this be a gentle reminder that healing doesn't mean forgetting; it means

Grief and Grace
learning to carry your grief with grace as you move forward.

You are stronger than you think. You are more resilient than you realize. And you are not alone.

Take one more deep breath. You've made it this far. You are here. You are capable. And you are loved.

Keep going — one step, one day, one moment at a time.

5 minute journaling

ONE THING I WANT TO REMEMBER ABOUT TODAY

_____
_____
_____
_____
_____

TODAY I FELT...

_____
_____
_____
_____
_____

TODAY I'M GREATFUL FOR

_____
_____
_____
_____
_____

5 minute journaling

ONE THING I WANT TO REMEMBER ABOUT TODAY

_____
_____
_____
_____
_____

TODAY I FELT...

_____
_____
_____
_____
_____

TODAY I'M GREATFUL FOR

_____
_____
_____
_____
_____

5 minute journaling

ONE THING I WANT TO REMEMBER ABOUT TODAY

TODAY I FELT...

TODAY I'M GREATFUL FOR

Manufactured by Amazon.ca
Bolton, ON